Just As I Am....

Written By: DRIA G.

Sitting here reminiscing about life's journey

Some times in life we need to relax, unwind, and think about how blessed we really are. This book speaks volumes is so few words. As you read through this book, make it your own personal journey by reading between the lines and realize how truly blessed you are.

As you go about your day, take the time
out to jot down the good times and even
the bad times. Jot down things you wish
you had done, things you could have
done, and things you would have done
differently.
Happiness
Jotting down the things that made me happy.

SELF
LOVE
SHE
CONQUERS
Reminding myself
that self love will
conquer all.

As you reminisce about your day's journey, always believe that your day has a very meaningful purpose.
Always remember that you have a purpose!!
REMEMBER YOUR WHY

If you don't believe in yourself, how can you expect anyone else to believe in you?
growth
Believing in myself is the beginning of my growth

must learn to focus on the goal set, not what others want or say.

Even though times may seem hard always be kind to yourself.

ME FIRST
Always put me first!! You matter!!

Family good. Bills paid. Bank account looking better. Healthy. No drama. Dreams coming true. Blessed. Thankful. Grateful.

Thank GOD !!

The main goal in life is to stay focussed on God first and always focus on yourself.
FOCUSED ON ME
My goal is to stay focused on me.

SHH..
I'M WRITING
write
on

Be kind to
yourself

No Greater feeling!
God is about to open doors, block distractions, renew your mind, and give you back your peace.

All in a day's work!!
FOR MY PEACE
I DELETE
I BLOCK
I DISOWN
I LEAVE
I IGNORE

Get out and see what the world holds for you.

There will always be times that seem unbearable. Just remember never give up. Things will get better!!!

NEVEr GIVE UP

You Never Know how Strong You really are Until being Strong is Your only Option
you ARE Strong
I AM Strong
strong!
The strong never walks along!!